Roadmaps for Multiplayer Success

The Evolution of Multiplayer Games

The evolution of multiplayer games showcases a remarkable journey driven by rapid technological advancements and shifting player expectations, shaping the very foundation of modern gaming experiences. Initially confined to local networks and arcade machines, multiplayer gaming ignited the spirit of competition with iconic titles like Pong, released in 1972, and Space Invaders, which debuted in 1978. These games established the multiplayer concept and set the stage for future developments, breathing life into interactive competition. The emergence of home consoles, such as the Atari 2600 in the late 1970s, and personal computers in the 1980s opened a world of possibilities, leading to the rise of LAN (Local Area Network) parties in the 1990s. These gatherings created a sense of camaraderie, where friends connected their machines to engage in unforgettable adventures across classic titles like Doom and StarCraft.

The transition to online gaming in the early 2000s marked a revolutionary moment in the industry, as widespread high-speed internet connections shattered geographical barriers, allowing players to connect and compete globally. Massively Multiplayer Online Games (MMOs) like EverQuest, launched in 1999, and Counter-Strike, initially released in 1999 as a mod for Half-Life, not only popularized this genre but also legitimized competitive gaming as a vibrant form of entertainment. This monumental shift presented new challenges for product managers, who now face the complexities of server management, robust player matchmaking systems, and the nurturing of thriving online communities.

As the gaming landscape evolved, so did player expectations. The sudden rise of social media platforms like Tik Toc and Facebook and streaming services such as Twitch fundamentally transformed interactions between gamers and developers. Community feedback became integral to game development, highlighting players' desires and grievances. This dynamic fueled a shift towards agile development methodologies, where continuous updates, player involvement, and real-time engagement became essential for fostering loyalty and active participation among players. Product managers responded by embracing community input, seamlessly integrating it into their development cycles to create responsive and fulfilling gaming experiences.

The advent of free-to-play models further revolutionized the multiplayer gaming paradigm, significantly lowering barriers to entry for new players. Games like Fortnite, launched in 2017, and League of Legends, which debuted in 2009, exemplified a successful fusion of accessibility and innovative monetization strategies, enabling developers to reach vast audiences without requiring an upfront purchase. This evolution prompted a more iterative approach to game design, where regular content updates, events, and seasonal changes were informed by actual player behavior and preferences. Product managers found themselves balancing creativity and innovation with the vital necessity of player satisfaction.

Today, multiplayer games continue to forge ahead with groundbreaking technological advancements, including cloud gaming services like Google Stadia and virtual reality platforms like Oculus

Rift. These innovations unlock new opportunities for product managers, encouraging the creation of immersive gaming experiences that leverage the cutting-edge capabilities of modern hardware. Moreover, the increasing emphasis on cross-platform play and inclusivity in gaming culture compels product managers to consider diverse player bases as they develop their roadmaps. By understanding the rich historical context and current trends in multiplayer gaming, product managers can navigate the exciting challenges of bringing successful multiplayer titles to life —titles that resonate deeply with players and nurture vibrant, engaged communities.

Key Roles in Game Development

In the vibrant and ever-evolving world of game development, a diverse array of key roles collaborates to shape the future of multiplayer games. Each role carries distinct responsibilities that propel the project from a mere concept to a remarkable reality, requiring creativity, strategic planning, and technical expertise. Understanding these roles is essential for product managers, as effective collaboration with these talented individuals is crucial to crafting comprehensive product roadmaps that lead to success. The primary roles in this ecosystem include game designers, developers, artists, sound designers, and quality assurance testers, each playing a pivotal part in the development cycle to steer the final product's overall direction and quality.

Game and narrative designers serve as the visionaries of the team, tirelessly conceptualizing engaging gameplay mechanics, compelling storylines, and unforgettable player experiences. They create the foundational blueprint that guides the development efforts, intricately detailing how players will interact within the game world and with one another. Effective game designers possess a deep understanding of player psychology and market trends, which enables them to develop captivating game loops that keep players invested over time. Product managers must work closely with game designers to optimize this process, aligning the product roadmap with the envisioned player experience while integrating community feedback into design iterations to ensure relevance and appeal.

Often regarded as the game's architects, developers are responsible for breathing life into the vision through programming and technical implementation. They translate design concepts into functional code, crafting the critical systems that enable seamless gameplay. A skilled team of developers tackles various technical challenges, ensuring optimal performance across multiple platforms, from consoles to PCs and mobile devices. As a product manager, facilitating effective communication between designers and developers is vital. This ensures that the original vision is realized while allowing for adjustments based on real-time community feedback, thus keeping the product closely aligned with player expectations and technological advancements.

Artists play a crucial role as the creators of the visual identity that captivates and immerses players in the gaming experience. They design unforgettable characters, breathtaking environments, and intuitive user interfaces that enhance the overall aesthetic. The art team collaborates closely with game designers to ensure that visual elements complement and enrich gameplay mechanics and narrative arcs. Product managers should champion this collaboration, facilitating dialogues between artists and designers and maintaining consistency across the aesthetic and experiential aspects of the game. Harnessing community feedback regarding visual preferences can significantly influence artistic direction and elevate player satisfaction, ensuring the game resonates deeply with its audience.

Sound designers add a profound layer of immersion through their expertise in audio mastery, skillfully crafting music, sound effects, and voiceovers that enhance the gaming experience. Their contributions are essential for evoking emotions and enriching the overall atmosphere of gameplay. Like their counterparts, sound designers must collaborate diligently with the entire team to ensure that audio elements seamlessly integrate with the gameplay experience. Product managers should actively embrace community feedback on audio, recognizing that players often have strong opinions about sound design. By combining this feedback into the product roadmap, the development team can create a genuinely engaging and satisfying player experience, which is critical for the success of any multiplayer game, ultimately fostering a loyal player base and encouraging community engagement.

Challenges in Multiplayer Game Development

The development of multiplayer games is an exhilarating journey filled with unique challenges that product managers bravely navigate to achieve successful outcomes. Foremost among these hurdles is the intricate realm of networking and server architecture. Unlike single-player games that rely solely on local resources, multiplayer experiences necessitate a robust and resilient infrastructure capable of supporting numerous simultaneous connections. This entails the meticulous configuration of servers that can dynamically scale based on player demand, ensuring low latency and unwavering stability. Product managers collaborate closely with technical teams to tackle this demand, leveraging cloud services and load-balancing techniques while implementing redundancy measures to prevent downtime. This endeavor requires a deep understanding of networking protocols, server management, and a proactive mindset to foresee and mitigate potential pitfalls, transforming these challenges into opportunities for enhanced player satisfaction and loyalty.

Another critical challenge resides in the delicate art of balancing gameplay to accommodate players' diverse skill levels and play styles. Multiplayer games create a vibrant and varied community that attracts individuals from casual players to hardcore enthusiasts with unique preferences. By prioritizing community feedback through surveys and playtesting sessions, product managers can pinpoint areas for gameplay adjustments, thus fostering an inclusive environment where every player can thrive. This iterative process involves frequent testing and meticulous analysis of player behavior data, enabling the continuous refinement of game mechanics, matchmaking algorithms, and progression paths. Striking the right balance is paramount; a well-crafted experience empowers players and significantly enhances their emotional investment and connection to the game.

Engaging with the community and integrating player feedback are foundational pillars for the successful development of multiplayer games. Product managers are tasked with establishing effective channels for players to voice their opinions and concerns, whether that be through dedicated forums, social media platforms, or in-game feedback systems. This dynamic interaction transforms challenges into a rich tapestry of insights that align with the overarching product roadmap. By prioritizing changes based on community input, product managers demonstrate a profound commitment to the game's vision and employ available resources strategically for impactful implementation, fostering a sense of ownership and investment within the player base.

Maintaining player retention amidst the ever-evolving landscape of multiplayer gaming is another thrilling challenge that product managers enthusiastically confront. With new games launching astoundingly, sustaining player engagement through compelling and evolving content becomes crucial. Ongoing content updates, such as seasonal events, themed expansions, and player-driven initiatives, are essential for rekindling interest and excitement. By developing a strategic roadmap that clearly outlines content delivery schedules, product managers ensure their teams are equipped to provide fresh and engaging experiences regularly. Product managers can analyze player engagement metrics—such as session duration, active user counts, and retention rates—to uncover critical trends that guide future content strategies and gameplay enhancements, supporting a dynamic, responsive game environment that keeps players returning.

Lastly, addressing the potential for toxicity and negative interactions within multiplayer spaces is imperative for cultivating a positive community atmosphere. Product managers collaborate closely with designers and community managers to implement robust moderation tools and comprehensive community guidelines. They establish systems that encourage positive interactions among players and actively deter toxic behavior, fostering a safe environment where every player feels valued and respected. Balancing player freedom by enforcing community standards becomes a commendable mission—whether that involves automated reporting mechanisms, player education initiatives, or facilitated conflict resolution strategies. Success in this realm not only enriches the overall player experience but also cultivates a loyal community that significantly contributes to the long-term triumph and sustainability of the game.

Defining a Product Roadmap

Defining a product roadmap is not merely a step in the game development process; it represents a crucial journey, particularly for multiplayer games where player experience and community engagement are paramount. A product roadmap serves as a strategic beacon, illuminating game development's vision, priorities, and progress over time. It transcends a rudimentary list of features or tasks, encapsulating the overarching goals and milestones that unite the development team and stakeholders in a shared mission. Through a well-articulated roadmap, product managers empower everyone to embrace a common understanding of the game's direction, an essential component for maintaining focus and momentum throughout the development cycle.

The cornerstone of a successful product roadmap is rooted in an understanding of the audience and their aspirations. For multiplayer games, this process entails engaging with the community early and often, effectively inviting players to participate actively in the game's developmental journey. Product managers must research extensively to uncover deeper insights into player preferences, pain points, and desired features. Various methods— surveys, community forums, social media interactions, and player interviews—can yield invaluable data that shapes the roadmap's strategic path. This community feedback helps direct feature prioritization and fosters a sense of ownership among players, significantly enhancing their loyalty and investment in the game's success.

Once insights are gathered, product managers can transform these into actionable items on the roadmap. This critical process involves prioritizing features and content based on their potential to enrich player experience and elevate community engagement. Striking a delicate balance between addressing popular requests and maintaining a cohesive long-term vision for the game is essential. Each item on the roadmap should carry a clear, defined purpose, whether to refine gameplay mechanics, enhance social features, amplify narrative depth, or address technical challenges. By establishing this clarity, the team can collaborate and effectively pursue shared objectives, ensuring everyone understands the "why" behind each roadmap item.

Incorporating flexibility into the roadmap is another vital element. The gaming industry thrives dynamically, with trends and player preferences continually evolving. A successful roadmap should function as a living document, adaptable to ongoing community feedback and market shifts. Product managers can weave in regular review points—perhaps every quarter—to assess progress, gather additional insights, and make necessary adjustments. This iterative approach ensures the game remains relevant and aligned with player expectations. It allows the team to pivot quickly in response to unforeseen challenges, such as changes in player sentiments or unexpected technological advancements.

Lastly, communication is the lifeblood of a product roadmap in multiplayer game development. Product managers must make sure that the roadmap is not only accessible but also resonates with all stakeholders, including developers, marketing teams, and the community at large. Transparent communication cultivates trust and inspires team collaboration, enabling everyone to contribute meaningfully to the game's vision. Regular updates on progress, challenges, and shifts in prioritization keep community engagement vibrant and support the overall development process. By crafting a well-structured, clear, and evolving product roadmap and communicating its essence effectively, product managers can navigate the complexities of game development while unlocking the full potential of multiplayer success.

Exploring the Essentials of Roadmaps for Multiplayer Games

When crafting compelling multiplayer games, product managers have a vital task: creating roadmaps that guide development and foster a thriving player community. Think of these roadmaps as a well-designed treasure map, each type crafted with a specific goal, steering the game through its various phases. The most prominent types include strategic, tactical, release, and community-centric roadmaps.

Strategic Roadmaps are like the north star of your game's journey. They illuminate a long-term vision, weaving together aspirations and goals that unite everyone involved—from developers to marketers. These roadmaps lay the groundwork for a bright future, aiming to boost player engagement and refine monetization strategies to ensure the game captivates its audience for years.

Tactical Roadmaps translate that grand vision into actionable steps, focusing on shorter-term initiatives that keep momentum. Product managers can tackle feature releases, balancing updates, and exciting promotional events here. This adaptable approach means they can pivot quickly based on player feedback and audience trends, ensuring the game remains vibrant and aligned with gamers' ever-evolving expectations.

Then, we have Release Roadmaps, which act as a guiding light for the exciting rollout of new content and features. These roadmaps lay out precise timelines, helping players anticipate eagerly awaited updates, expansions, or significant patches. In the fast-paced world of multiplayer gaming, timing is everything. A well-structured release roadmap influences player retention and community engagement, seamlessly syncing marketing efforts and announcements so players are always in the loop and buzzing with anticipation.

Community-centric roadmaps are emerging as game-changers in the development landscape. By weaving player feedback directly into the fabric of the roadmap, these tools empower the community to shape the game's trajectory. Through surveys, discussions on forums, and engagement on social media, product managers can craft a roadmap that genuinely reflects the desires and needs of the player base. This collaborative approach builds players' fierce sense of ownership, fostering loyalty and connection.

What makes all these roadmaps truly powerful is their ability to harmonize. A comprehensive product roadmap for a multiplayer game beautifully intertwines elements from all four types. By combining strategic, tactical, release, and community-centric perspectives, product managers create a dynamic roadmap that drives development and nurtures a strong bond with the player community. This holistic approach ensures the game evolves harmoniously with both developers' visions and players' aspirations, setting the stage for continued success in the realm of multiplayer gaming.

The Power of a Well-Structured Roadmap

A well-structured roadmap is more than just a tactical instrument for product managers in the game development industry; it serves as a vital beacon of vision and direction for the entire development team, particularly within the complex landscape of multiplayer games. It harmonizes the efforts of diverse roles—from designers and programmers to marketers and community managers—by aligning all members with the project's strategic goals, thereby creating a cohesive force dedicated to a shared purpose. The roadmap promotes transparency and communication by outlining a comprehensive timeline that includes feature releases, updates, and critical milestones essential for thriving in the intricate world of multiplayer systems. This clarity mitigates misunderstandings and engenders a collaborative spirit that fuels creativity and drives innovation.

One of the standout strengths of a

well-structured roadmap is its capability to inspire meticulous planning and prioritized execution. In the ever-evolving realm of multiplayer game development—where player engagement, community feedback, and competitive dynamics are paramount —the roadmap enables product managers to pinpoint and prioritize features significantly enhancing the player experience. For instance, a roadmap could delineate phases for implementing core gameplay mechanics, aesthetic improvements, and community-requested features, ensuring that resources are allocated judiciously. This strategic prioritization allows teams to tackle the most critical elements, ensuring the development process remains agile and focused. By proactively anticipating player needs and aligning these with broader business objectives, product managers can architect a user experience that captivates players and fosters long-term retention and loyalty.

Integrating community feedback into the roadmap is another decisive advantage. Multiplayer games flourish on the strength of vibrant player communities, making it vital for developers to be responsive to their needs and suggestions. A structured roadmap actively embraces community insights by incorporating mechanisms for feedback—such as surveys and discussion forums—thereby allowing the game to evolve harmoniously with its audience. By regularly updating the roadmap based on this player feedback, product managers cultivate trust within the community, instilling a sense of ownership among players that inspires deeper engagement and investment in the game's success.

Moreover, a well-structured roadmap excels in managing expectations for the development team and the players. Product managers reduce the uncertainty and anxiety inherent in the game development process by providing a detailed outline of what to expect and when—complete with specific timelines, feature descriptions, and potential impact on gameplay. This proactive communication strategy fuels momentum and keeps teams focused on their objectives while ensuring that players feel informed and engaged throughout the development journey, thereby enriching their overall gaming experience.

Finally, a well-structured roadmap is a dynamic, living document that evolves alongside the game. In the fast-paced and often unpredictable gaming industry, a flexible roadmap empowers product managers to adapt to new trends, emerging technologies, and shifting player behaviors. This adaptability is critical for the long-term success of multiplayer games, as it allows teams to pivot effectively while maintaining strategic focus. By regularly revisiting and updating the roadmap—including revising timelines based on the development pace and incorporating new insights from player interactions—product managers can ensure that their development efforts remain relevant and impactful, leading to a more prosperous and sustainable gaming experience that resonates with players long after launch.

Setting Clear Objectives and Goals

Setting clear objectives and goals is vital in crafting a comprehensive product roadmap for multiplayer games. These objectives form the bedrock of the development process, guiding teams in their decision-making and feature prioritization. For product managers, defining these objectives requires a profound understanding of the game's vision, target demographic, and community expectations. A well-articulated set of objectives aligns the team's collective efforts, ensuring that all members work toward a unified purpose while optimizing resource allocation across various stages of development.

In establishing objectives, weaving together both short-term and long-term aspirations is crucial. Short-term goals, typically spanning a quarter to a year, emphasize immediate features that enhance gameplay, address bugs, or respond to community feedback. These could include rolling out a new matchmaking system or introducing seasonal events that invigorate user engagement. Conversely, long-term goals reflect the overarching vision of the game and its evolution over several years, such as expanding the game universe, introducing new modes, or significantly enhancing graphics and mechanics. This dual focus not only fuels team motivation but also guarantees that the roadmap remains relevant and adaptable to the ever-changing desires of players and market dynamics. By regularly revisiting and refining these objectives—at least once per quarter—product managers maintain a clear direction through the uncertainties of game development.

Community feedback serves as a cornerstone in shaping objectives and goals. Engaging players through diverse channels—surveys, forums, beta tests, and social media platforms—reveals invaluable insights into their expectations and experiences, including preferred gameplay mechanics or desired content updates. This continuous dialogue informs the prioritization of features and enhancements within the product roadmap, ensuring that the development process resonates deeply with the target audience. By actively integrating community feedback, product managers cultivate a sense of ownership among players, strengthening their loyalty and enhancing long-term player retention.

When setting objectives, defining measurable outcomes is equally important. Utilizing key performance indicators (KPIs), such as player engagement rates (e.g., daily active users), session length, retention statistics (e.g., 30-day retention), or community satisfaction scores (gathered from direct feedback or net promoter scores), empowers product managers to track progress and evaluate the impact of their strategies. For instance, if an objective is to increase player retention by 15% over the next six months, clear metrics provide a basis for assessing whether changes yield results. These measurable outcomes highlight successes and create a roadmap for recalibrating efforts and strategies as needed.

Ultimately, setting clear objectives and goals is an ongoing journey that demands flexibility and responsiveness. As the game improves and the community grows, product managers must be prepared to revisit and refine their objectives regularly. This iterative approach ensures that the roadmap remains aligned with player expectations and the overarching vision for the game. By fostering a culture of continuous improvement, product managers can deftly navigate the complexities of game development, leading their teams toward multiplayer success while maintaining a strong connection to the gaming community.

Identifying Target Audience and Market Research

Identifying the target audience is a crucial journey for product managers in the game development sector, mainly when crafting innovative product roadmaps for multiplayer games. A comprehensive understanding of your players' identities empowers you to tailor game features, marketing strategies, and community engagement initiatives to meet their needs and preferences. A well-defined target audience can range from casual gamers who may enjoy quick and accessible gameplay to hardcore enthusiasts who often seek depth, complexity, and competitive engagement in their gaming experiences. Each segment possesses unique characteristics, motivations, and expectations that can significantly influence game design and development processes.

To effectively segment your

audience, consider analyzing various factors, including demographics (age, gender, geographical location), gaming habits (platform preferences, average playtime, types of games favored), and psychographics (lifestyle, values, interests). This nuanced segmentation allows you to prioritize features that resonate deeply with each player group, ensuring a more engaging and fulfilling gaming experience tailored to their preferences.

Market research is essential in this identification process, involving robust gathering and analysis of data about potential players, existing competitors, and prevailing industry trends. To conduct thorough market research, implement effective methods such as surveys with targeted questions, focus groups for deep qualitative insights, and data analytics to track player behavior patterns. Analyzing player feedback from beta tests or early access releases yields valuable information about desirable features, mechanics that resonate with players, and areas needing enhancement. Furthermore, conducting competitive analysis provides a clearer picture of what similar games offer, helping you identify existing market gaps that your game can fill, ultimately positioning it for tremendous commercial success.

Integrating community feedback is equally crucial in identifying and refining the target audience. Engaging with players through dedicated forums, social media platforms, and in-game feedback mechanisms fosters a vibrant and interactive community. Encouraging open dialogue and actively listening to player suggestions, critiques, and concerns grants firsthand insights into their preferences and values. By incorporating this feedback into the product roadmap, you enhance player satisfaction and instill a sense of loyalty; players feel heard and valued throughout the development process. This iterative approach to product development significantly increases the game's appeal and longevity.

Moreover, leveraging analytics tools allows tracking player engagement and behavior over time, providing valuable quantitative data that complements qualitative feedback. Metrics such as player retention rates, average session lengths, in-game purchasing patterns, and player demographics reveal crucial insights that inform key decisions about feature prioritization and gameplay adjustments. By continuously monitoring these metrics, product managers can adapt their roadmaps in response to evolving player behavior, thus ensuring the game grows harmoniously with audience expectations and prevailing market trends. This dynamic and responsive approach is essential for maintaining relevance within the fast-paced and ever-changing landscape of multiplayer gaming.

In conclusion, identifying the target audience and conducting comprehensive market research are foundational steps in the game development journey. Product managers can forge a product roadmap that aligns seamlessly with both players' needs and market opportunities by harmonizing qualitative feedback, quantitative analytics, and proactive community engagement. This strategic alignment elevates the overall gaming experience and fuels long-term success in an increasingly competitive industry landscape, ensuring the continuous growth and adaptation of the game within its genre.

Prioritizing Features and Functionality in Multiplayer Games

Prioritizing features and functionality is a vital step toward crafting a remarkable product roadmap for multiplayer games. As product managers, it is crucial to deeply understand and embrace the unique needs of your audience. Through comprehensive player research and data analysis, you can identify essential features that deliver maximum value and significantly enhance their gameplay experience. Establishing this groundwork sets the stage for long-term success in an increasingly competitive gaming landscape.

A systematic approach to prioritization involves employing a scoring system that rigorously evaluates potential features against a diverse set of criteria, including player impact, development effort, technical feasibility, and alignment with the overarching goals of the game. For instance, features that directly improve gameplay mechanics or offer novel experiences might score higher in player impact, while those requiring extensive resources might rank lower in feasibility. This quantitative assessment empowers product managers to gauge the relative value of each feature effectively, paving the way for informed and strategic decision-making.

In multiplayer games, assessing how features foster community engagement and social interaction takes on heightened importance, as these elements are pivotal in driving player retention and satisfaction. Features such as party systems, social hubs, or integrated voice chat can significantly enhance the social fabric of the game. Prioritizing functionalities that encourage teamwork and interaction cultivates a robust player community, ultimately leading to longer player lifecycles and more vibrant in-game ecosystems.

Community feedback serves as an essential tool in the prioritization process. Actively engaging players through structured surveys, interactive forums, and social media discussions can yield valuable insights regarding their preferences and pain points. For example, players may express a desire for specific in-game improvements or new content types that resonate with their experiences. By attentively listening to the community, product managers can pinpoint the most desired features and address functionalities that may be lacking. This direct communication not only fosters goodwill but also illustrates a genuine commitment to providing what players truly want, thereby enriching the overall gaming experience and promoting loyalty.

In addition to harnessing community feedback, analyzing the competitive landscape proves vital when prioritizing features. By scrutinizing successful titles within the genre, product managers can discern industry trends and identify features that resonate effectively with players. For instance, if rival games successfully implement dynamic event systems or seasonal content, these insights can guide your priorities in a way that maintains relevance and draws inspiration from successful models. A strategic approach to feature selection not only helps maintain competitive parity but also allows for carving out a unique niche that distinguishes your game amid a crowded marketplace.

Lastly, the prioritization process should maintain an iterative and flexible nature. As the game expands, and the player base grows, fresh insights, fluctuating player demands, and emerging trends will necessitate a reevaluation of established priorities. Regularly revisiting the roadmap—perhaps on a monthly basis —can facilitate adjustments based on ongoing community feedback, analytical metrics, and market shifts. By adopting an adaptable mindset and being open to change, product managers can ensure that the features and functionalities being developed are continually aligned with the dynamic needs of players and the broader objectives of the game. This unwavering commitment to an informed and responsive prioritization process is essential for achieving sustained success in the vibrant realm of multiplayer gaming.

The Role of Community in Game Development

The role of community in game development is a pivotal force in crafting successful multiplayer games. Communities are vibrant ecosystems, brimming with diverse perspectives, experiences, and insights that significantly shape every stage of the development journey. For product managers, fostering an ongoing dialogue with these passionate players unlocks a wealth of opportunities to enhance the game's design, functionality, and overall player experience. By nurturing a spirit of collaboration and inclusivity, product managers can effectively align their product roadmaps with the aspirations and interests of their player base, ultimately leading to increased player satisfaction and retention.

Engaging the community starts with establishing open and direct channels of communication. This can take place through various platforms, including social media networks (such as Twitter, Discord, and Facebook), official game forums, and dedicated feedback tools like surveys and suggestion boxes. By creating safe havens for players to express their opinions, share experiences, and suggest improvements, developers cultivate a strong sense of belonging within the community. This engagement goes beyond merely collecting feedback; it nurtures relationships that inspire players to invest emotionally in the game. When players feel that their voices are valued and heard, they often blossom into enthusiastic advocates, actively promoting the game and sharing their positive experiences with others.

Integrating community feedback is essential for sculpting a cohesive and responsive product roadmap. Product managers must carefully analyze insights gathered from community interactions to identify recurring patterns and prioritize features that resonate most strongly with players. By systematically categorizing feedback into actionable insights, they can align community-driven priorities with the game's overarching vision and objectives. This strategic alignment ensures that the requested features are thoughtfully addressed, reflecting player input while enhancing overall satisfaction and fostering a sense of ownership within the community.

Moreover, community involvement profoundly influences the iterative approach that is so crucial in multiplayer game design. Continuous feedback loops enable product managers to test new features, mechanics, and gameplay elements with community members during various development phases. Involving players in alpha and beta testing not only fine-tunes gameplay mechanics but also builds palpable excitement and anticipation surrounding upcoming releases. When communities perceive themselves as integral stakeholders in the development process, it significantly bolsters loyalty and energizes the entire game ecosystem.

Lastly, recognizing and rewarding community contributions deepens the connection between developers and players, reinforcing the collaborative spirit that drives successful game development. Acknowledgment of top contributors can take various forms, such as including their names in game credits, offering exclusive in-game items, or hosting special community events and competitions. Celebrating the essential role that the community plays in a game's success not only honors their contributions but also cultivates a shared sense of purpose. In the fiercely competitive realm of multiplayer gaming, a robust and dedicated community can transform the landscape, not only providing unwavering loyalty but also serving as an invaluable wellspring of innovation and creativity that propels the game forward into new realms of possibility.

Methods for Gathering Community Feedback

Gathering community feedback is an essential and empowering step in developing multiplayer games, as it consistently aligns the product roadmap with the hopes and aspirations of the player base. By effectively collecting feedback, we can significantly enhance the development process, leading to a more captivating and enjoyable player experience. Product managers are encouraged to implement a diverse range of strategies to capture a rich tapestry of community sentiments and preferences, ensuring that all voices are heard and considered.

Surveys and questionnaires have emerged as powerful tools for gathering insights. Product managers can obtain quantitative data that illuminates player preferences and pinpoints pain points by designing targeted surveys that delve into specific aspects of the game—such as gameplay mechanics, narrative elements, or user interface. Utilizing online platforms like Google Forms or SurveyMonkey for distribution enables broad participation across diverse player demographics, fostering a collection of varied opinions. To maximize engagement, it's crucial to keep surveys concise and focused, ideally consisting of a mix of multiple-choice questions and open-ended prompts. This approach encourages higher response rates and ensures that actionable insights guide the product roadmap.

Community forums and social media platforms are exceptional venues for gathering real-time feedback. Product managers gain immediate access to player concerns, suggestions, and even community-driven content by actively engaging with players on platforms like Reddit, Discord, and Twitter. This engagement cultivates a vibrant community, encouraging players to voice their thoughts openly and constructively. Moreover, these platforms can facilitate AMAs (Ask Me Anything) sessions or focus group discussions, creating interactive opportunities for more in-depth qualitative feedback. These discussions can uncover nuanced player sentiment and build stronger relationships between developers and the community.

In-game feedback tools also serve as an effective method for collecting player input directly within the gameplay experience. Players can effortlessly share their thoughts while immersed in the game by integrating intuitive feedback mechanisms—such as a dedicated feedback button or pop-up surveys. This might include options for submitting bug reports, feature requests, or general feedback through an easily accessible interface. Such tools simplify communication and enable product managers to gather data at critical moments, ensuring that player input is both relevant and immediate. Furthermore, analyzing the context in which feedback is given can provide deeper insights into player experiences.

Finally, beta testing and early access programs are crucial in gathering community feedback before a release. By inviting selected players to explore new features, game mechanics, or entire game builds, product managers can directly observe in-game interactions and solicit direct feedback through structured interviews or surveys following gameplay sessions. This method is invaluable for assessing how well the game aligns with player expectations, revealing strengths and improvement opportunities. Integrating player feedback during these testing phases can profoundly influence the final product roadmap, ensuring that the game evolves harmoniously with its community and resonates with a broader audience upon full release. By actively listening and responding to player input at all stages of development, we can create multiplayer experiences that truly reflect the desires and needs of our players.

Embracing Feedback as a Path to Greatness

Analyzing and implementing feedback stands as a pivotal journey in developing a successful multiplayer game. For product managers, this journey begins with the courageous act of actively collecting input from players across various platforms, interpreting their sentiments, and weaving their insightful ideas into the product roadmap. By accurately deciphering community feedback—whether through comments in forums, reactions on social media, or data from in-game surveys—developers can dramatically steer the trajectory of the game, ultimately forging a final product that resonates deeply with player expectations and market demands. In the ever-evolving gaming industry, where player preferences shift at lightning speed, a flexible and responsive approach to feedback is not just essential; it becomes a hallmark of excellence that can distinguish a game within a crowded marketplace.

The adventure truly begins with establishing a robust feedback collection system. This involves a multifaceted approach: utilizing structured surveys that target specific areas of gameplay, engaging with players on popular social media platforms like Twitter and Discord, cultivating vibrant forums where discussions can flourish, and creating intuitive in-game feedback mechanisms that allow players to contribute suggestions at key moments. Product managers should prioritize these channels' accessibility and user-friendliness, ensuring players of all backgrounds can easily share their thoughts. Product managers can gather a treasure trove of insights that genuinely reflect players' experiences, preferences, and aspirations by actively nurturing community engagement and creating an environment where players feel valued and heard.

Once the data is in hand, the analysis phase unfolds in earnest. This phase is marked by the meticulous categorization of feedback into recognizable themes while also discovering broader trends that may exist within the community. Product managers should seek quantitative data, such as player ratings and numerical survey scores, and the qualitative richness of player comments to paint a comprehensive picture. Leveraging advanced tools like sentiment analysis can gauge emotional nuances in player feedback, providing invaluable insights into community sentiment regarding specific game elements, gameplay mechanics, story arcs, or character designs. With this synthesis of data, product managers can illuminate the path forward, identifying features that resonate most with players and highlighting the areas ripe for enhancement or reimagining.

The real challenge, however, emerges in the implementation of feedback. Product managers must carefully prioritize suggestions based on feasibility, anticipated impact, and alignment with the game's overarching vision and goals. This process often presents tough choices, as not all feedback can be embraced simultaneously—balancing immediate player desires with long-term growth strategies is crucial. Communicating with the community regarding which suggestions will be realized and offering insightful context on why specific ideas may not fit within the current development cycle fosters transparency, builds trust, and ignites further engagement from the player base.

Ultimately, the realization of feedback should be embraced as an iterative journey, not a one-time event. Product managers should diligently monitor the effects of changes implemented based on community input, remaining poised to adapt further as additional feedback pours in or as player dynamics shift. This dynamic dialogue between developers and players is vital for nurturing a thriving game ecosystem. By consistently revisiting and refining the product roadmap in response to community feedback, product managers can ensure the game evolves in ways that meet and exceed player expectations and drive sustained engagement and long-term success in the exhilarating landscape of multiplayer gaming.

The Agile Approach to Game Development

The Agile approach to game development is a dynamic and iterative methodology that emphasizes flexibility, collaboration, and the incorporation of customer feedback throughout the creative journey. Unlike traditional, linear development methods—where planning, execution, and delivery follow a rigid sequence—Agile enables teams to iterate rapidly, adapt to changing demands, and provide incremental updates that can significantly influence the gaming landscape. This adaptability is particularly transformative in the domain of multiplayer games, where player feedback serves as a crucial element in refining gameplay mechanics and enhancing the overall user experience. By encouraging an environment focused on continuous improvement, Agile empowers product managers to shape their product roadmaps effectively and engage meaningfully with the gaming community in real-time.

At the core of Agile lies the concept of sprints—short, focused phases of development that typically last from one to four weeks. During each sprint, teams concentrate on specific tasks or features, allowing for the delivery of functional game elements in manageable increments. For product managers, this means creating roadmaps that outline the game's long-term vision and incorporate regular checkpoints for evaluating progress, assessing team outputs, and integrating community feedback. By systematically incorporating player insights after each sprint, development teams can prioritize features that resonate most with users, ensuring that the game evolves in alignment with community expectations while remaining committed to achieving development goals.

Cross-functional collaboration stands

as a foundational principle of the Agile methodology. In the context of game development, this spirit of collaboration requires developers, designers, product managers, and community managers to unite in sharing insights, brainstorming solutions, and tackling challenges collectively. Product managers play a vital role in fostering this synergy, ensuring that all team members remain aligned with the game's vision, objectives, and overall goals. This vibrant collaborative environment not only sparks creativity and innovation among team members but also streamlines decision-making processes, allowing for speedy responses to market shifts, emerging trends, and player feedback.

The integration of community feedback serves as a vital heartbeat of the Agile approach, especially in multiplayer games where player engagement and satisfaction are paramount. By proactively seeking input from the player base through methods such as surveys, online forums, alpha and beta playtests, and community discussions, product managers can gather invaluable insights that inform the development roadmap. This feedback loop gives teams the agility to promptly address player preferences and pain points, refining the game experience to reflect the community's desires and aspirations. Agile methodologies encourage product managers to perceive this feedback not just as information, but as an essential resource that cultivates a sense of community ownership and investment in the game's evolving journey.

In essence, the Agile approach to game development equips product managers with a robust and adaptable framework to create product roadmaps that prioritize player engagement and responsiveness. By leveraging the structure of sprints, nurturing a collaborative atmosphere, and continuously integrating community feedback, product managers can navigate the intricate landscape of multiplayer game development with greater confidence and efficacy. This proactive stance not only elevates the quality of the game but also fosters a loyal player community that feels heard and valued, ultimately laying a strong foundation for lasting success in the dynamic and vibrant world of gaming.

Embracing Community Feedback for Inspiring Game Development

Adjusting roadmaps based on community feedback is not merely a routine task; it is a critical journey in the game development process, especially for multiplayer games that thrive on community engagement and interaction. Product managers have a unique opportunity to transform their games by actively soliciting input from players at various stages of development, ensuring that their creative vision aligns with user expectations and aspirations. This commitment to listening empowers product managers to identify trends, preferences, and pain points that illuminate the path forward, leading to a dynamic, responsive product roadmap and a more rewarding gaming experience for players.

Establishing clear and consistent communication channels is essential when integrating community feedback into the development roadmap. By leveraging platforms such as dedicated game forums, popular social media channels, and comprehensive in-game surveys, product managers can collect valuable insights directly from their audience. The subsequent analysis of this feedback, carefully categorizing it into actionable items ranging from minor tweaks to major feature requests, becomes a powerful tool for prioritizing changes that resonate with the overarching vision of the game while addressing the community's most pressing concerns. This strategic focus on prioritization not only cultivates player engagement but also nurtures a loyal community, eager to contribute further.

As product managers make adjustments to the roadmap, they must thoughtfully consider the timing and scope of proposed changes. Implementing too many drastic alterations in a single update can overwhelm both the development team, disrupting workflow and productivity, and the player base, leading to confusion and frustration. Instead, a focus on incremental updates—such as rolling out one or two significant features at a time, complemented by smaller quality-of-life improvements—helps facilitate gradual enhancement while effectively managing player expectations. Regular updates, no matter how minor, not only keep the community engaged and informed but also reinforce their commitment to the game's ongoing evolution.

To amplify the impact of feedback integration, creating a robust feedback loop is an invaluable strategy. This cyclical process transforms the relationship between developers and players; it involves not only acting on feedback but also proactively communicating how player input shapes the product roadmap at every stage. This transparency fosters trust and cultivates a strong bond between the community and the development team. When players can see their suggestions leading to tangible, meaningful changes—such as new game mechanics, balanced gameplay adjustments, or additional content—it inspires more individuals to engage in the feedback process. This creates a vibrant cycle of communication and ongoing improvement, enhancing community involvement and satisfaction.

In essence, adjusting development roadmaps based on community feedback is an imperative practice in the ever-evolving realm of multiplayer game development. By fostering open communication, prioritizing player feedback, embracing gradual, incremental changes, and maintaining transparency, product managers can craft a roadmap that genuinely reflects the desires and needs of the player base. This collaborative spirit not only elevates the player experience but also lays the groundwork for the game's lasting success and relevance in a competitive market. This alignment with the community ensures that the game continually resonates with players, encouraging longevity and engagement over time.

Internal Communication with Development Teams

Internal communication with development teams is the heartbeat of successful product management in the game development industry. When communication flows effectively, every team member becomes aligned on project goals, timelines, and responsibilities— essential elements that cultivate productivity and help achieve milestones. For product managers, comprehending the dynamics of internal communication is key to streamlining processes and nurturing an environment rich in creativity and innovation. By leveraging tools like project management software (such as Jira or Trello), regular stand-up meetings, and collaborative platforms (like Slack or Discord), product managers can maintain open lines of communication that fuel the exchange of ideas and feedback among development teams.

Establishing clear channels of communication is vital for seamless coordination among various departments such as design, programming, and quality assurance (QA). Product managers have the opportunity to implement structured communication protocols, including scheduled update meetings (weekly or bi-weekly), ensuring that everyone remains aligned with the project's current status and goals. This approach not only aids in tracking progress but also empowers team members to swiftly identify potential challenges, allowing for proactive solutions. Creating an inclusive atmosphere where team members feel encouraged to voice their opinions and suggestions fosters an engaged workforce, ultimately leading to the creation of exceptional products that resonate with players.

Incorporating community feedback into the development process is another pivotal aspect of effective internal communication. Product managers can facilitate vital discussions that illuminate player expectations and concerns related to the game's roadmap. These discussions may include regular surveys, forums, or beta testing groups that gather player insights, preferences, and pain points. By synthesizing and sharing insights gathered from community feedback sessions, product managers guide their teams in prioritizing features that resonate deeply with players. This two-way communication cultivates a collaborative culture where development teams are empowered to make design decisions that reflect player desires, thereby enriching the overall user experience.

Additionally, utilizing visual aids such as project roadmaps and timelines significantly enhances internal communication. These tools vividly illustrate the project's status, key milestones, and overarching vision, making it easier for all team members to understand their roles within the broader context of the game's development lifecycle. Regularly updating these visual aids not only instills a sense of accountability but also serves as a motivational tool, as team members witness their progress toward shared goals. Moreover, these references can serve as focal points during meetings, ensuring that discussions remain engaging, productive, and focused on actionable outcomes.

Finally, nurturing a culture of continuous improvement through feedback loops is vital for sustaining effective internal communication. Product managers are encouraged to invite development teams to share their insights on the communication processes themselves, facilitating a transparent environment that allows for meaningful adjustments and refinements. By consistently evaluating the effectiveness of communication strategies —through retrospectives and surveys— product managers can identify opportunities for enhancement that bolster collaboration and cohesiveness. This iterative approach not only strengthens relationships within the team but also contributes to the triumphant success of the game development project, ensuring that the final product beautifully aligns with both the intended vision and the aspirations of the community it serves.

External Communication with the Community

External communication with the Community is a crucial pillar of effective product management in multiplayer game development. Active engagement with players fosters a strong sense of belonging and provides invaluable insights to inform product roadmaps. An effective communication strategy, built on the right channels and clear, targeted messages, nurtures meaningful interactions that enhance player loyalty and satisfaction, ultimately aligning development efforts closely with the aspirations and desires of the Community.

To create a robust communication framework, product managers should first identify the most effective platforms for connection. Social media outlets such as Instagram, alongside forums like Reddit and dedicated Discord servers, present rich opportunities for dialogue. Each platform has its own special characteristics and user expectations, which require tailored strategies for effective engagement. For instance, Twitter thrives on concise, real-time updates and fast-paced interactions that capture immediate reactions. In contrast, community forums provide a space for in-depth discussions, where players can share elaborate insights and experiences. Understanding where the Community congregates and their preferred modes of communication allows for outreach to evolve into a powerful tool for fostering engagement and connection.

Transparency serves as a cornerstone for establishing trust within the gaming community. Regular updates on game development, including progress on new features, bug fixes, and any challenges faced by the development team, empower players to feel actively involved in the game's evolution. Clear communication about timelines and milestones nurtures a sense of partnership between developers and players, encouraging constructive feedback that can directly influence the product roadmap and enhance the overall gaming experience.

Feedback collection should not be viewed as a one-time event; rather, it should be a continuous journey. Product managers should proactively seek player input through various channels, including surveys, polls, and open discussions during community events such as livestream Q&As or gaming conventions. This active engagement not only gathers a wide range of perspectives but also reassures players that their opinions are valued and impactful. When feedback is not only recognized but also embraced, it strengthens the Community's role as a crucial force in shaping the game, inspiring more players to share their thoughts and contribute to a continuous cycle of improvement and innovation.

Finally, the analysis of feedback and the practice of closing the loop with the Community is paramount. Following the collection of insights, product managers should take the initiative to communicate how this feedback influences decision-making within the development process. Sharing results through blog posts, video updates, infographics, or community meetings reinforces the notion that player input is foundational to the game's evolution. This practice not only enriches community relations but also establishes a solid groundwork for future communication and feedback initiatives, ensuring that the voices of players remain a vital cornerstone of the product roadmap, ultimately fostering a thriving, engaged player community.

Tools for Roadmap Visualization

Effective roadmap visualization acts as a cornerstone for product managers in the dynamic realm of game development, particularly in the complex domain of multiplayer games. The right tools not only empower the translation of strategic goals into clear, actionable plans but also ensure those plans resonate deeply with both the development team and the gaming community. By leveraging various visualization techniques, product managers can illuminate the strategic path forward, ensuring that every stakeholder—from developers to investors to players—fully comprehends the roadmap and its essential role in achieving success.

One of the most revered tools for roadmap visualization is the Gantt chart. These charts allow product managers to methodically outline project timelines, key milestones, and interdependencies. By visually plotting tasks along a timeline, teams can quickly identify critical paths and potential bottlenecks. This clarity is particularly invaluable in multiplayer game development, where seamless coordination among design, programming, quality assurance, and marketing teams is imperative. Gantt charts can also be customized to incorporate specific phases for community feedback, ensuring that player insights actively influence the product's evolution throughout its development lifecycle.

Another powerful tool is the Kanban board, which offers a flexible and interactive workspace for visualizing work in progress. Utilizing a Kanban board allows product managers to categorize tasks into distinct stages, such as "To Do," "In Progress," and "Completed." This methodology not only nurtures transparency within the team but also fosters open communication among team members. As community feedback pours in

—ranging from bug reports to feature requests—these insights can be swiftly transformed into actionable tasks on the board, enabling the development team to prioritize based on real-time player input. This level of visibility ensures that the roadmap remains agile and responsive to the continuously evolving needs of both the team and the gaming community.

Mind mapping software significantly enhances the process of roadmap visualization as well. It encourages product managers to brainstorm and visually organize ideas, thereby crafting a comprehensive overview of the game's development process. Mind maps can reveal critical features and gameplay elements that warrant inclusion in the product roadmap while also seamlessly accommodating community feedback. By vividly illustrating the interconnections and hierarchies of various game components— such as character development, level design, and user experience—product managers can ensure that all relevant voices are acknowledged and integrated, leading to a more cohesive and engaging product vision.

Lastly, interactive roadmap tools like

Trello or Aha! provide a dynamic forum for collaboration and communication among team members and stakeholders. These platforms enable product managers to create digital roadmaps that can be effortlessly shared across the entire team and the broader gaming community. Features such as drag-and-drop functionality, real-time commenting, and the ability to attach files amplify collaborative efforts and facilitate ongoing dialogues about the roadmap's progression. By actively engaging the community in this process, product managers can gather invaluable insights and foster a sense of ownership among players, ultimately leading to a more immersive and satisfying multiplayer experience.

Inspiring Definitions of Key Performance Indicators

Key Performance Indicators (KPIs) are unique and essential tools for product managers navigating the dynamic landscape of multiplayer game development, particularly when formulating product roadmaps tailored for engaging player experiences. These measurable values shed light on how effectively a team or company is achieving its critical business objectives, serving as a compass for strategic decision-making. In multiplayer game development, identifying the right KPIs enables teams to monitor progress meticulously, make informed, data-driven decisions, and synchronize development efforts with the evolving expectations of players and the diverse feedback from the gaming community.

When establishing KPIs for multiplayer games, it is crucial to prioritize metrics that reflect both player engagement and the overall health of the game. Commonly used KPIs in this vibrant sector include Daily Active Users (DAU), which measures the number of unique players engaging with the game each day; Monthly Active Users (MAU), which provides insight into engagement over a longer timeframe; player retention rates, indicating how well the game keeps players returning over days, weeks, or months; and average session length, which tracks how long players spend in the game during each play session. Monitoring these indicators allows product managers to evaluate the effectiveness of current features, assess player interest, and identify areas that warrent improvement or innovation.

In addition to engagement metrics, product managers should actively incorporate KPIs that gauge community sentiment and player feedback. Metrics such as the Net Promoter Score (NPS), which reflects player likelihood to recommend the game to others; comprehensive player satisfaction surveys that gather qualitative and quantitative data; and levels of community engagement across forums, social media platforms, and in-game channels are invaluable for understanding player perceptions and attitudes. These KPIs not only reveal how many players are actively participating but also provide crucial insights into how players feel about their gaming experience. By integrating community feedback into the product roadmap, developers can align their efforts with player desires, leading to enhanced satisfaction and loyalty.

Moreover, it is quite essential for product managers to regularly reassess and adapt their KPIs as the game evolves. As new features are introduced, or significant updates occur, the relevance and weighting of certain metrics may shift dramatically. For instance, upon the launch of a new game mode, it becomes vital to establish specific KPIs that measure its success, such as participation rates, player completion statistics, and direct player feedback regarding that mode. This level of adaptability enables product managers to maintain an acute focus on the most pertinent aspects of game performance and player engagement.

Ultimately, the effective definition and implementation of KPIs can significantly enhance the decision-making process for product managers in the realm of multiplayer game development. By thoughtfully selecting the right metrics, embracing community feedback as a core component of development strategy, and maintaining a flexible approach to performance measurement, teams can craft product roadmaps that not only fulfill business objectives but also resonate deeply with players. This strategic alignment paves the way for sustained success in a thriving, competitive gaming landscape, fostering a loyal player base and securing a reputable position in the market.

Tracking Progress Against the Roadmap: A Comprehensive Approach

Tracking progress against the roadmap is crucial for ensuring that a multiplayer game development project remains on course and excels in its execution. As product managers, you bear the responsibility of curating a cohesive and transparent view of the project's journey. The process begins with the establishment of precise, measurable milestones that align with your roadmap. These milestones should be specific, achievable, and time-bound, enabling both qualitative and quantitative evaluations of progress. By way of example, setting a milestone for the completion of the game's core mechanics by a specific date allows the team to gauge their pace effectively. Regularly reviewing these milestones illuminates potential bottlenecks or areas that may warrent adjustments or additional resources, thereby ensuring the development team remains focused on the overarching vision of the game.

The integration of project management tools significantly enhances the efficiency of the tracking process. Platforms such as Trello, Jira, or Asana provide intuitive visual representations of progress, facilitating seamless task updates and clarifications on responsibilities. By leveraging these tools, product managers can create dashboards that showcase real-time statistics on various aspects of the game development cycle, including task completion rates, bug resolution status, and overall project health. This level of transparency fosters an environment of collaborative accountability among team members. Additionally, scheduling regular check-ins, such as bi-weekly stand-up meetings or sprint reviews, creates opportunities to discuss ongoing progress, identify bottlenecks, and celebrate significant milestones, ultimately cultivating a positive and motivated team culture.

Community feedback emerges as an invaluable asset in shaping the development of multiplayer games. As you track progress, it is essential to integrate player insights into your roadmap actively. Establishing diverse channels for community feedback, such as dedicated forums, online surveys, or social media engagement campaigns, allows you to gather crucial insights regarding player experiences, preferences, and expectations. For example, conducting post-beta testing surveys can reveal players' thoughts on gameplay mechanics and their impact. Analyzing and prioritizing this feedback within the roadmap ensures that player needs and desires are consistently met throughout the development process. By remaining responsive to community input, product managers can make informed decisions that enhance player satisfaction and engagement, ultimately steering the game towards a more successful launch.

Periodic evaluations of the roadmap are essential in adapting to the rapidly evolving gaming landscape and the shifting expectations of players. Given the dynamic nature of the industry, influenced by emerging trends, technological innovations, and changes in player behavior, consistently revisiting the roadmap provides insights into areas ripe for modification. This proactive approach enables the incorporation of new ideas, features, or expansions that can enhance the game's appeal and keep it relevant in a competitive market. For instance, if a new gaming technology is gaining traction, considering its integration into the development plan could attract a wider audience.

Lastly, effective communication serves as the heartbeat of tracking progress against the roadmap. Keeping all stakeholders—including team members, upper management, and even community advocates—well-informed fosters an environment of trust and collaboration. Regular updates delivered through structured meetings, informative reports, or engaging newsletters contribute to maintaining high levels of engagement and enthusiasm among all parties involved. As product managers, nurturing open lines of communication makes sure that everyone is in line with the current project status, future goals, and any challenges that may arise. This collective awareness not only elevates team morale but also aligns efforts towards shared objectives, ultimately setting the stage for a triumphant multiplayer game launch that resonates with players and stands out in the market.

Adjusting Strategies Based on Metrics

Adjusting strategies based on metrics is a foundational pillar of product management in multiplayer game development. Metrics provide critical insights into understanding player behavior, engagement levels, and overall game performance, acting as a guiding light for decision-making. By meticulously analyzing these insights, product managers can identify areas of strength and opportunities for growth, enabling them to craft experiences that resonate with player expectations and align with market trends.

One of the primary metrics to focus on is player retention. Understanding the percentage of players who return after their initial session is essential for evaluating the effectiveness of onboarding processes and game mechanics. For instance, if retention rates drop below 40% in the first week of gameplay, it signals an urgent need to reevaluate and enhance the onboarding experience. Product managers can tackle this challenge by redesigning the onboarding sequence, improving tutorial interactivity, or altering gameplay mechanics to ensure that new players are not only engaged but also equipped to enjoy the game fully. Initiatives like introducing reward mechanisms for returning players can further bolster retention rates.

Engagement metrics, including average session length and the frequency of play, are vital for shaping impactful product strategies. High engagement levels, such as players logging in for an average of 2 hours a day and participating in daily challenges, often correlate with higher player satisfaction. Features that captivate the audience—like seasonal events or limited-time challenges—can spark increased engagement. Conversely, if there's a noticeable decline in session length, such as dropping from an average of 90 minutes to 40 minutes per session, it becomes critical to unleash creativity for new content or gameplay refinements. Product managers should cherish these insights and leverage them to inform content updates, feature enhancements, and promotional campaigns that reignite player enthusiasm, contributing to a vibrant gaming community.

Community feedback is an invaluable ally in the process of adjusting strategies based on metrics. Product managers should actively engage with the player base through surveys, community forums, and social media platforms to gather qualitative insights that complement quantitative data. For example, if metrics indicate a dip in user engagement following a major update and community feedback reveals players are struggling with a new control scheme, this constructive feedback allows product managers to address specific pain points directly—perhaps reverting certain changes or providing additional tutorials on the new mechanics.

Finally, adopting an iterative approach when adjusting strategies based on metrics is crucial for long-term success. The gaming landscape is perpetually evolving, with player preferences shifting as new trends emerge. Regularly reviewing performance data alongside community feedback facilitates a proactive stance, allowing product managers to remain agile and responsive to player needs. By continuously refining the product roadmap with these insights and implementing frequent updates, teams can ensure their multiplayer games not only meet player expectations but also thrive in an increasingly competitive market. This iterative cycle fosters a culture of innovation and responsiveness that keeps players invested and excited about the game.

Successful Roadmaps from Leading Companies in the Gaming Industry

Successful roadmaps from leading gaming companies offer invaluable insights into the intricate art of planning and executing multiplayer game development. These industry trailblazers have established best practices that significantly elevate product quality while igniting robust community engagement. By examining their strategies in detail, product managers can uncover powerful techniques to craft impactful roadmaps that prioritize player feedback and seamlessly adapt to the ever-evolving dynamics of the gaming market.

A prime example is Riot Games, which is globally recognized for its iconic title, League of Legends. Their product development roadmap is intricately shaped by community feedback, which they systematically gather through an array of channels, including active online forums, detailed player surveys, interactive social media platforms, and direct engagements at community events and conventions, such as PAX and the League of Legends World Championship. This comprehensive feedback loop empowers Riot to prioritize features and enhancements that genuinely resonate with their player base, ensuring both relevance and satisfaction. They make it a point to transparently highlight upcoming changes through regular communication, including patch notes and town hall meetings, while providing extensive content outlines in advance. This commitment cultivates a profound sense of ownership among players, promoting a more engaged community and nurturing long-term loyalty.

Blizzard Entertainment showcases another impressive strategy with a nuanced phased approach to roadmapping, particularly evident in their popular team-based shooter, Overwatch. Their roadmap distinctly breaks down development timelines into short-term (1-3 months), medium-term (3-6 months), and long-term (6 months or more) goals. This structure allows them to swiftly respond to player feedback while consistently delivering substantial updates that enrich gameplay. To maintain transparency, Blizzard regularly updates players on the status of anticipated features and enhancements through developer blogs and community Q&A sessions. This not only sets clear expectations for players but also builds excitement and anticipation, significantly enriching the overall player experience and reinforcing community trust.

Epic Games stands out through its relentless commitment to community feedback with Fortnite. Their agile development process facilitates rapid iterations based on player suggestions and comprehensive gameplay data analytics, leveraging tools like player metrics and heat maps. Regular updates—often on a weekly basis—introduce new features, limited-time events, crossovers with popular franchises, and balance changes—all directly informed by player input. This agile responsiveness keeps the game vibrant and dynamic, demonstrating to the community that their voices are truly valued. The result is a deeper player investment, heightened satisfaction, and a unified community that feels actively involved in the game's ongoing evolution.

Finally, Ubisoft's roadmaps for titles like Rainbow Six Siege highlight the power of merging a long-term vision with active community involvement. They regularly share future plans encompassing seasonal updates, major content drops, operator releases, and community challenges in in-depth developer updates. Furthermore, they host community events—both online and in-person—where players can directly communicate their experiences, concerns, and feedback to developers, often through forums and roundtable discussions. This approach not only strengthens the bond between developers and the community but also ensures the game evolves in harmony with player expectations and desires.

By drawing inspiration from these formidable companies, product managers can design comprehensive roadmaps that not only deliver exceptional content but also cultivate a thriving multiplayer gaming ecosystem. This ultimately leads to a more satisfied and loyal player base, fostering long-term success in the competitive gaming landscape.

Lessons Learned from Roadmap Failures in Game Development

Roadmap failures in game development often serve as pivotal learning experiences for product managers, especially within the dynamic and highly competitive landscape of multiplayer games, where sustained community engagement is vital for long-term success. One of the most significant lessons learned from these failures is the importance of setting realistic timelines and milestones that align closely with the actual capabilities and resources of the development team. When product managers implement overly ambitious schedules—perhaps influenced by market pressure or heightened competition—it can lead to team burnout, increased turnover rates, and hasty or incomplete feature rollouts. Such a situation ultimately frustrates players, who may feel neglected or disappointed by the quality and stability of the game. To mitigate these risks effectively, product managers should prioritize establishing clear, achievable goals that are tailored to their team's capacity and available resources, allowing for a sustainable development cycle. This approach not only facilitates sufficient time for necessary iterations but also encourages continuous community feedback, making it possible to refine features based on user input before their public release.

Another essential takeaway from these experiences is the critical importance of incorporating community input into the planning and development process. In numerous instances, product managers have faced considerable backlash after launching features that were misaligned with player expectations; such missteps often result in negative reviews, diminished player engagement, and, ultimately, a downturn in player retention rates. By actively speaking with the community through a variety of communication channels—such as detailed forums, comprehensive surveys that gauge player sentiment, and organized beta testing groups—product managers can identify potential issues early within the development cycle. This proactive approach enables timely adjustments based on real-time player feedback, significantly enhancing overall player satisfaction and fostering a sense of ownership and loyalty among users who feel their voices are genuinely heard and valued throughout the developmental process.

Flexibility is another cornerstone highlighted by past failures. Roadmaps should be regarded as living documents, adaptable to the rapidly changing landscape of player preferences, technological advancements, and emerging industry trends. Product managers must embrace an agile mindset, continuously refining their plans based on real-time data drawn from player interactions, community sentiments, and thorough industry analyses. Regular check-ins—such as weekly team meetings to assess progress and monthly roadmap reviews to realign objectives—empower the development team to pivot as needed without losing sight of the overall project vision. This adaptability is crucial to maintaining relevance in a competitive marketplace and meeting the ever-evolving expectations of players.

Effective communication within both the development team and the player community is fundamental in ensuring clarity and preventing misunderstandings that could lead to further roadmap failures. Clear and consistent messaging regarding project expectations, shifts in direction, and regular progress updates are vital to nurturing both team dynamics and the community's perception of the development process. Product managers should prioritize transparency, sharing both successes and challenges candidly, fostering an atmosphere of trust and collaboration. Communities that are well-informed tend to be more supportive of a product manager's decisions—even when unexpected obstacles arise—as they feel a sense of belonging in the journey and a vested interest in the outcomes.

Finally, conducting thorough analyses of past roadmap failures can lead to more informed decision-making for future projects. By performing in-depth post-mortems on initiatives that did not meet their objectives, product managers can pinpoint specific pain points, recurring issues, and miscalculations that thwarted success. This reflective practice enables teams to craft targeted strategies designed to mitigate similar risks in upcoming roadmaps. By instilling a culture that focuses on learning from mistakes and celebrating continuous improvement, teams can enhance their overall effectiveness. This ultimately leads to the creation of more resilient roadmaps that tightly align with both business goals and community needs, emphasizing the necessity for adaptive strategies within the competitive landscape of multiplayer game development. This thoughtful approach paves the way for more successful, player-centric outcomes, increasing the chances of achieving lasting engagement and satisfaction within the gaming community.

Key Takeaways for Product Managers in Multiplayer Game Development

Product managers play an instrumental role in shaping the direction and success of multiplayer games. One takeaway is the importance of creating a comprehensive product roadmap that harmonizes the game's strategic vision with the community's needs and desires. A well-defined roadmap serves as a guiding document outlining the essential features, updates, and milestones necessary for delivering a successful multiplayer experience. It should clearly delineate short-term and long-term goals, including timelines for each phase of development, anticipated player engagement metrics, and key performance indicators (KPIs). Additionally, it is essential for product managers to ensure that the roadmap aligns with the overarching goals of the game while being flexible enough to adapt to evolving player feedback and market dynamics.

Another critical aspect for product managers is the integration of community feedback into the product roadmap. Gamers are not just passive consumers; they are often deeply invested in their experiences and can provide invaluable insights that help shape the future of the game. Establishing diverse channels for gathering feedback—such as in-game surveys, dedicated forums, social media interactions, and community events—enables product managers to create an ongoing dialogue with the player base. This fosters a sense of ownership and community among players, leading to deeper engagement. Encouraging player input can culminate in identifying key areas for improvement and innovation, which in turn can drive higher levels of player satisfaction and retention, as players recognize that their voices are being heard and actively considered in the game's development.

Moreover, prioritization is an essential skill for product managers when developing a roadmap. With finite resources—including budget, personnel, and time—it is critical to ascertain which features and updates will yield the most significant impact on player satisfaction and engagement. Product managers should employ qualitative and quantitative methods to evaluate potential features, taking into account factors such as player demand measured through analytics, technical feasibility assessed by engineering teams, and alignment with the overall game vision articulated during the concept phase. This prioritization process should not be static; it should be revisited regularly to ensure that the roadmap remains relevant and responsive both to ongoing player needs and shifts in market trends.

Collaboration with cross-functional teams represents another vital takeaway for product managers in the game development journey. The successful execution of a product roadmap hinges on input and support from diverse departments, including design, engineering, marketing, and community management. By actively fostering a collaborative environment through regular meetings, brainstorming sessions, and the use of management tools, product managers can ensure that various perspectives are factored into decision-making, leading to a more well-rounded and effective roadmap. Addressing potential roadblocks early in the development process through open communication helps synchronize efforts across teams and mitigate delays in launching updates or new features.

Finally, product managers should adopt a mindset of continuous learning and adaptation. The gaming landscape is continually evolving, influenced by shifting player preferences, emerging technology, and industry trends. By remaining informed through market research, attending gaming conferences, and engaging with thought leaders, product managers can refine their strategies. Regularly assessing the effectiveness of the product roadmap and making data-driven adjustments—such as reallocating resources based on player engagement trends or enhancing features that receive high player feedback—enables product managers to enhance their approach and ensure the long-term success of multiplayer games. This commitment to evolution not only benefits the product manager but ultimately leads to a richer and more rewarding experience for players, fostering a loyal and engaged community.

Developing Your Roadmap

Creating a comprehensive roadmap is essential for bringing your multiplayer

game to life and ensuring its ultimate
success. A thoughtfully structured product
roadmap guides the team's vision and
objectives, prioritizes vital features, and
integrates invaluable community feedback
throughout the development lifecycle.
Start with a clear set of goals that embody
your creative aspirations and resonate
deeply with your target audience—this
could include enhancing player
engagement, fostering a vibrant
community, or achieving specific sales
targets. Conduct thorough market
research to understand player
expectations, analyze competitor offerings,
and identify gaps and opportunities in the
market. Establish key performance
indicators (KPIs), such as user retention
rates, daily active users (DAU), and player
feedback scores, to measure success at
various stages of development.

With objectives firmly in place,
outline the major phases of the game
development lifecycle—pre-production,
production, beta testing, launch, and post-
launch updates. Each phase should have
clearly defined milestones, such as concept
art completion in pre-production, alpha
builds in production, or targeted feedback

sessions during beta testing. This clarity illustrates progress and enhances team members' communication, which makes sure everyone is aligned with the goals. By segmenting the development process into manageable, well-defined steps, product managers can efficiently allocate resources, track individual and team responsibilities, and celebrate achievements while remaining open to adjustments based on timely community insights.

Incorporating community feedback is paramount to crafting a game that genuinely connects with its audience. Engage with players through various platforms—dedicated forums, social media channels, and organized playtesting sessions—to gather profound insights into their preferences, gameplay experiences, and challenges faced. Establish a systematic approach for collecting, analyzing, and prioritizing this feedback, including leveraging surveys, suggestion boxes, or feedback tracking tools. Creating a dedicated channel for community contributions not only creates a sense of ownership and investment among players but also enhances loyalty and advocacy.

Prioritizing features and updates is crucial for a successful roadmap. Product managers must balance community desires, technical feasibility, and overarching business objectives harmoniously. Employing frameworks like the MoSCoW method (Must have, Should have, Could have, Would like) empowers informed decision-making about which features to prioritize. This decision-making process should remain flexible, allowing for adaptations based on continuous community input and evolving market dynamics. Additionally, conducting regular reviews of the backlog and updates can ensure that the development process stays responsive to player needs.

Finally, communication serves as the lifeblood of effectively executing the roadmap. Regularly updating all stakeholders, including team members and the player community, cultivates transparency and builds trust. Product managers can leverage digital roadmapping tools, such as Trello or Aha!, to visualize progress, set deadlines, and share updates in real-time. Frequent check-ins, team meetings, and structured feedback sessions ensure that everyone remains informed and engaged, thereby reinforcing the bond between the development team and the community. By respecting these principles, product managers can craft a dynamic and adaptable roadmap that not only guides the development process but also elevates the overall player experience, leading to a more successful and sustainable game.

Resources for Continued Learning in Game Development

Embracing a commitment to lifelong learning is essential for product managers in the ever-changing landscape of game development. Staying ahead of trends, new technologies, and best practices is key to crafting compelling product roadmaps for multiplayer games. Various platforms, including online courses, webinars, and industry conferences, offer invaluable insights tailored to the unique challenges of the gaming industry.

Online learning platforms like Coursera, Udemy, and LinkedIn Learning feature a diverse array of courses specifically tailored for game development and product management. These courses cover critical topics such as agile methodologies, user experience design, and community management—knowledge essential for product managers who integrate community feedback into their roadmaps. By harnessing these resources, product managers can deepen their understanding of the game development lifecycle and effectively prioritize features based on player input.

Participating in webinars and virtual workshops presents a great opportunity learn from industry experts. These events often spotlight current trends, case studies, and best practices directly applicable to product management in gaming. Networking during these sessions can lead to meaningful connections, fostering knowledge exchange and collaboration that enrich a product manager's toolkit.

Industry conferences like the Game Developers Conference (GDC) and PAX serve as immersive environments for learning and growth. Attending these events allows product managers to engage with thought leaders, uncover the latest tools and technologies, and take part in hands-on sessions that address real-world scenarios. The insights gained here can significantly enhance the development of product roadmaps and enable the integration of community feedback through the diverse perspectives encountered.

Finally, leveraging online communities and forums is a powerful way to stay informed and connected. Platforms like Reddit, Discord, and dedicated game development forums are vibrant spaces for discussions on product management and community engagement strategies. By actively engaging with players, product managers can learn from the challenges faced by their peers, ultimately enhancing their ability to create effective product roadmaps that truly resonate with the multiplayer gaming audience.

www.ingramcontent.com/pod-product-compliance
Lightning Source LLC
La Vergne TN
LVHW051745050326
832903LV00029B/2742